Is Abortion Murder?:

Respecting Human Life.

By

George Burbach

CONTENTS

Introduction

There are several questions to be asked about the subject of abortion. Most of the books and articles concerning abortion are written by women and have a woman's point of view. That reflects the often assumed that abortion is a woman's issue, not a mens issue.

This book concerning abortion is written from the perspective of a man, a man who has been personally involved with abortion. I know from personal experience that men seldom feel any responsibility when their sex partner has an abortion performed.

Every effort is made to tell it like it is, not how some people would like it to be. There is no candy coating. The book includes the issues of birth control, euthanasia, death penalties, and other things concerned with human life. It is about the often forgotten need to respect human life.

Chapter One

What is Abortion?

To abort something is to stop something that has already begun. So9 when we discuss human abortion. Were are talking about stopping a human life while it is already in the process of living/ At the instant the sperm enter the egg in the woman's uterus, a human life begins. It is a biologically complete human being or biological entity.

Theologically, at that instant of conception, Almighty God breathes another soul into existence in the body of the child, which we refer to as the fetus. The fetus is a whole and complete human being, body and soul. It I like a seed that has been planted in the ground. When the seed germinates, it starts to grow. First some roots and then a sprout, and then as the sprout emerges out of the soil, it grows and matures into a plant. As a plant, it grows and eventually produces seeds which then are planted and more plants grow from those seeds. The conception of a human being is much the same. The egg is fertilized by the sperm and the human begins to grow. First, within the mother's uterus, and then, like the plant that emerges from the soil, it s expelled from the uterus and grows and matures and procreates to produce more humans.

The problem for people who try to justify abortion is that they cannot accept the biological reality of human conception. We are biological entities with spiritual souls. At the moment of conception. We are not just a glob of protoplasm that turns magically into a human being at the time of birth or expulsion of the "glob" from the uterus.

Self justification is a major flaw of all humans. We want to always be right, even in the face of proof that we are wrong. A fetus is a human being with all the right to life as all other human beings. No one has a right to kill him or her.

Chapter Two

Why is it legal if it is murder?

Hitler did not think that killing the Jews in the gas chambers or with firing squads was murder either. The rest of the world considered him a "Mass Murderer." He did kill six million people.

Abortion has killed 52,000,000 people in the last forty years in the United States alone. That is murder too. Mass murder on a much, much larger scale than Mr. Hitler's 6,000,000 Jews. Neither of the perpetrators thought it was murder but it was. They killed other human beings.

No doctor comes out of the operating room saying, "*Oh boy, I justifiably killed another human being again*". No mother says how happy she is that she just killed her baby.

Abortion should be called just what it is, justifiable, legal murder of another human being. Why don't the supporters of abortion say that. Could it be that they know the truth and cannot admit it? Instead they invent all sorts of rational reasons to support their explanation justifying their actions.

They are obviously very convincing in their arguments and were able to get the laws passed to legalize their position. Just because it became the law of the land, it doesn't change the reality and it doesn't change God's Commandment, "Thou shalt not kill." Hitler legalized killing the Jews too and that didn't change the rest of the world's reality that it was murder, plain and simple/ It broke the moral law and nothing Mr. Hitler said or did changed that fact. He had legalized murder for his own warped reasons.

Just call a spade a spade and don;t try and hide from it.

Abortion is murder.

Chapter Three

Who is responsible for having an abortion performed?

Everyone is responsible. The laws were passed by the majority of the population and so the burden of the responsibility falls on everyone, whether they are for or against it. If they are against it, they should take whatever legal means are available to change the law.

In the individual case, the mother, the father, and the person performing the abortion are responsible for the murder of the child. Of course the obvious person responsible is the pregnant woman. She does not want the child to come to full term and be birthed so she hat him or her killed.

The biological father may or may not know the woman is pregnant. He is responsible for getting the woman pregnant and therefore has a direct responsibility for the child whether he knows about the abortion or not. If he doesn't know about the pregnancy, he is still responsible for the child because he fathered him or her. That occurred for me once. The girl I had gotten pregnant had not told me she was and only after the fact, told me she had gotten pregnant and had gotten the baby killed.

The other situation in my life was when a married woman I had gotten pregnant told me about being pregnant and asked me what I thought she should do. Her husband was sterile, so she couldn't claim it was his child. I told her that I believed that abortion was murder, but she went to a lady who performed abortion and killed the child anyway.

I felt very guilty about both situations after I had gotten sober in AA. I really didn't think about them in my drinking years but when I took my Fourth Step moral inventory, there they were and I knew I had direct responsibility in both cases.

I have heard doctors who have performed abortion tell about having to kill the baby after it was removed from the uterus. They justified this by saying the mother had authorized the abortion and expected the unborn child to be dead. They felt no guilt for the murder they had performed.

The fetus is a whole and complete human being from the instant it is conceived. It is murder to kill another human being.

Chapter Four

Should your parents have had you aborted?

My mother, a raging alcoholic used to corner me and tell me repeatedly that I was just a ***"hole in a rubber"*** and that she and my Dad did never wanted kids. She wished I had never been born, but obviously I was. In those days, abortion was illegal and so people who did not want kids used whatever birth control methods were available. If they didn't work, then the woman had to have the baby, want him or her or not.

What if your parents didn't want you born. You were defenseless and were at their complete mercy. If that were today, your mother could have gone to the nearest abortionist and had you killed. You would not be alive today. Think about that. Next Mother's Day you should be extra nice to her and in some way thank here for letting you be born and allowing you to live.

The unique gift of procreation is probably the most important gifts that God bestowed man with.

God gave us the power to be co-creators of human life.

Many women who have had abortions are haunted by it the rest of their lives. They killed their baby and can never bring that person back to life, the life that God had intended to have lived in this world. Their conscience remains guilty and many of them end up in therapy trying to cope with their responsibility for the abortion

The women are not the only ones. The fathers feel the guilt also and many report it nagging at them throughout their own life. Many often do have to seek therapy or some way to remove their guilt and remorse. I know, I was one of them. I was blessed with the availability of confession. I know God has forgiven me the sin involved but, as the priest told me in the confessional, I have two children in heaven that I should pray for them and that they are there praying for me. their human father.

I also met one doctor who gave up the practice of Obstetrics because of his overwhelming guilt about killing so many children.

The practice and participation in abortion effects everyone involved. Whether a person approves or not, we all allow legalized abortion to exist. We still make euthanasia or mercy killing illegal and still do very little to protect the old and infirm.

Killing another human being is immoral and a clear

violation of God's Commandment:

Thou shalt not kill

Chapter Five

What is the morally correct position on abortion?

This is very simple. No person has the right to kill another person! There is no justifiable murder even though some forms of murder are humanly legal such as criminal executions, war, and the more common forms of murder, such as abortion. ABORTION IS MORALLY WRONG.

God did not create us to destroy the human life He has given to each person. He created life so that people could live and use and develop all of the gifts with which He has endowed each person.

ABORTION IS MURDER

Self Test

1. What is your personal position on the morality of abortion?

2. What is your position on the legality of abortion?

3. Would you help another person get an abortion if they wanted one?

If yes, why?

4. Have you ever actively opposed or supported abortion.

   What did you do?

5. If you have ever been involved in an abortion, write a letter to the mother telling her what you feel now about supporting her decision.

6. If you have had an abortion performed, write a letter to your unborn, dead child who is now in heaven with his or her heavenly Mother Mary, the Mother of God.

7. **What is your exact position on abortion today.**

8. What would you tell another person who wanted an abortion performed.

9. **What is your position on the entire subject you would be willing to tell anyone.**

10. What are your after thoughts?

Appendix

Bibliography